GETTING
TO
KNOW
YOUR
BIBLE

Getting
to
Know
Your
Bible

FORTRESS PRESS

Philadelphia

This book is a freely adapted translation by David L. Scheidt of the book by Hans-Georg Lubkoll and Eugen Wiesnet entitled *Wie liest man die Bibel? Eine Gebrauchsanweisung für Neugierige, Anfänger und Fortgeschrittene,* copyright © 1974 by Robert Pfützner GmbH, Munich, Germany, and published by Christophorus-Verlag Herder GmbH, Freiburg, Germany.

Library of Congress Catalog Card Number 75-34527

ISBN 0–8006–1217–5

5261K75   Printed in U.S.A.   1-1217

CONTENTS

PART ONE

What We Should Know about the Bible

A Book to Read or a Dust-Catcher?

According to reliable statistics more than 278 million Bibles and Testaments in 1500 languages were sold, distributed, or given as gifts in the year 1972. In Asia, Eastern Europe, Africa, and Latin America the demand for Bibles is so great that publishers and Bible societies are hard put to meet the demand. There the Bible is eagerly and conscientiously read.

But, strange to say, in the "Christian" world the Bible has become a best-selling dust-catcher. People buy the Bible and display it on their bookshelves or coffee tables. But the only acquaintance an increasing number of people have with the Bible's content is acquired from movie spectaculars and musicals such as *Godspell* or *Jesus Christ Superstar*.

To no little degree this widespread ignorance and neglect of the Bible is due to modern reading habits. So many people are accustomed to reading matter of a type entirely different from that found in the Bible. They find it rather easy to read light and frothy fare. They can read and grasp the language of tabloid newspapers, slick magazines, and paperback novels. But the kind of reading matter which requires the reader to think does not find too eager an audience.

It is, however, more likely that fewer people read the Bible now than formerly because reading the Bible requires us to enter into a peculiar world entirely different from the one in which we live. Not only is the biblical world different from our world, but the way in which the biblical writers thought is quite different from the way in which we think. To put it simply, the Bible reader must not only enter into another world—the world of antiquity—but also overcome a mentality gap that extends over more than two thousand years.

Nonetheless, not everything in the Bible is strange and alien to us. Though Bible readers find themselves on ancient, foreign soil and must grapple with a different world outlook and way of thinking, there is much in the Bible that is familiar. In the Bible we find men and women—people of flesh and blood as we are—struggling with the same problems and questions with which we struggle. That is one of the reasons the Bible is read so eagerly in lands where we would least expect to find it read at all.

It is the intention of this book to encourage and to help people who for the first time are making a serious attempt to read the Bible with understanding. Hopefully this book will provide not only the initiative to read the Bible, but also the kind of information and background that will enable one to read it with understanding and profit.

The Record of Experience

Contrary to what many people believe or simply take for granted, the Bible did not fall from heaven completely written from Genesis to Revelation. In fact, the book we know as the Bible consists of a number of books composed by a great many writers over a period of more than one thousand years. The intention of these writers was not to create a body of literature. In all probability they never dreamed that what they wrote would someday be regarded as Holy Writ and endowed with unique religious authority. It was, however, the intention of these writers to preserve and to pass on to succeeding generations a record of a people's experience of God.

In order to understand what this means, the Bible reader must know something of the mentality and outlook of the Near East of some three thousand years ago. There it was taken for granted that divine forces and powers were at work in the world. For the Babylonians these divine powers or deities were personified by the sun, the moon, and the stars. Egyptians conceived of these powers as supernatural beings and depicted them as having the heads of animals. The inhabitants of Canaan looked upon these forces and powers as the mysterious sources of the earth's fertility symbolized by the bull.

From these beliefs a number of ancient religions developed, all of which had one thing in common. That one thing was the underlying common belief that the gods can be found in nature and that they are part and parcel of the physical, natural world.

Such was not the case with the Hebrews, or as we call them today, the Jews. More than 1200 years before the birth of Jesus Christ this people, under the leadership of a man named Moses, made what at that time was a revolutionary confession of faith. They held that the one true God cannot be found *within* the realm of nature. Furthermore, this God is not identical with nature. On the contrary, God is the Lord of the world, beyond man's power to grasp in his fullness or to subject him to man's will and ends. Unlike the gods of their Near Eastern neighbors, the God of the Hebrews could not be "proved" or demonstrated as though he were a physical object or a force that could be manipulated. He is above and beyond man and nature.

Because of their concept of God the Hebrews were looked upon with suspicion and distrust by their neighbors, who often regarded them as godless atheists.

Under no circumstances, however, should the God of the Hebrews be construed as an abstract idea. For the Hebrews God was not an idea or a concept. He who is beyond man's grasp and understanding was the one whom their people experienced. It was this God who chose their small and insignificant nation to be his special servant, and to that end he led the Hebrews out of bondage in Egypt.

It is the experience of this divine act of deliverance that the authors of the Old Testament recount again and again. Indeed, this divine act of liberation was what constituted not only the

Hebrew nation and a recurrent Old Testament theme, but the fundamental experience of the God who, though he is above man, nonetheless acts in man's affairs in order to achieve his ends, not man's.

Note that the people's experience of God came first. The biblical record of that experience came afterward.

What is true of the Old Testament is also true of the New Testament. The experience which preceded the New Testament and caused it to be written was the resurrection of Jesus Christ from the dead. More than anything else it was the early Christians' stunning, shattering experience of Jesus' resurrection that threw a new and entirely different light upon the itinerant rabbi from Nazareth they called Lord.

At first the story of Jesus' message and of his triumph over the grave was communicated orally. But as the original witnesses to Jesus' ministry began to die off, the story and the message connected with it were put into writing. Here again it must be stressed that it was the experience of Jesus Christ and his resurrection which preceded the written word of the New Testament. This experience of Jesus and of his resurrection was so overwhelmingly powerful that those whose lives it gripped and regenerated could not be silent about what they had experienced; they had to share it through the spoken and written word.

The Biblical Writers: Their Purpose and Method

When one has gone through a harrowing, distressing situation one cannot speak of the experience in a detached, matter-of-fact way, as though one were giving a recipe or quoting prices on the daily stock-exchange listing. One tells of the experience in intense, personal, and vivid language. One relates what has happened with feeling and passion, zeal, and conviction. The experience is related not only in terms of what happened but in terms of what was felt, sensed, and realized. This is the way the writers of the Bible conveyed the message of their experience of God's truth and working. Their purpose in writing was to express and share their experience as compellingly and convincingly as possible.

This purpose may seem quite strange to novice Bible readers

who, for a host of reasons, often and wrongly have the impression that the sole function and purpose of the Bible's writers was to report what happened, what they had seen and heard, as exactly as possible. Such an impression probably has its roots in an idea prevalent in the nineteenth century that the historian's task is to research and report events as precisely and dispassionately as possible. The major flaw in this idea is that however accurately and precisely some event may be reported, such a report cannot possibly convey the motives and feelings which caused this or that event or series of events to take place. This idea of the historian's task can produce only a dry record of essentially barren words; it cannot reproduce or even suggest the vibrance of life, the heat and feeling of flesh and blood caught up in the struggles of life and living.

The writers of the Bible were not historians in the nineteenth-century sense of the word. They had no desire whatever to go into precise details as though they were composing legal documents intended to cover every exigency. This accounts, for example, for the lack of detail in the Passion and Easter stories. (The reason for the lack of details in the creation story in Genesis is obvious.)

The intention of the Bible writers was singular: to make it clear that God does not turn his back upon mankind. In effect, then, their writings were a form of preaching and exhortation to faith. Anything and everything else was secondary to that intention. In order to achieve their end these writers employed whatever literary vehicle served best. That is why we find such a wide variety of literary forms in the Bible: songs and hymns, letters, parables, folk tales, legends, military reports, speeches, accounts of scandal, geneologies, love poems, liturgical passages, and stories not unlike the short story of modern times. Each of these types of literary form was employed by the Bible's writers as a vessel to contain the message they sought so ardently to convey. From this method of the Bible's writers there accrues a distinct advantage to the modern Bible reader; namely, that somewhere in this book there are types of literary form which appeal and speak to the reader in such a way that he says to himself, "That's exactly how I feel."

An inkwell from Qumran on the Dead Sea.

Fact, Legend, Myth, and Truth

The primary concern of the Bible's writers to convey a message did not prevent them from mentioning specific historical events and facts. This was especially true where the writers themselves were involved in these events. In many instances their references to such events and facts have been confirmed and verified by extra-biblical authorities and sources. The Bible records the destruction of Samaria (722 B.C.), and so do Assyrian cuneiform tablets. Nor is the Bible the only record of Hebrew bondage in Egypt. Reference to the Hebrews is made on a column erected by one of the pharoahs. Babylonian tablets tell of the destruction of Jerusalem (587 B.C.). The Persian king Cyrus, mentioned in Isaiah 45, was anything but a legendary figure. From Roman historians we have evidence that Pontius Pilate ruled in Palestine from 26–36 A.D. and had his residence in the seaport city of Caesarea. Coins mentioned in the New Testament are on display in museums throughout the world. Werner Keller's well-known book *The Bible as History* relates a great many more incidents and shows that other matters mentioned in the Bible are corroborated by other authorities.

In view of what has been said previously, the reader must wonder why the Bible only mentions some particular historic events, but in other cases goes into unexpected detail. The answer is that the various Bible writers wanted to demonstrate that God is not an abstract idea or a figment of man's imagination. They wanted to demonstrate that the God who is above and beyond man works his will and way in the course of human history. That is precisely the point made by the unknown prophet who wrote Isaiah 45–55. Forcefully and without inhibition this prophetic writer interprets history from a theological point of view. For him historical events were not important in themselves. What was important for him was that in these events he saw evidence that God lays low and raises up, that he not only chastises but comforts and restores his faithful. This is a way of thinking to which the Bible reader must become accustomed. What this way of thinking asserts is that heaven, land, and sea are the Lord's, that rulers are his agents and history his teaching tool.

But while the Bible's writers mention much that is historical and which can be historically authenticated, they also include much material that is in the category of legend and myth. These two terms suggest to a great many people that whatever is designated as legend or myth is *ipso facto* not true, and for certain kinds of Bible readers such a thought is unbearable. This is not and need not be the case.

Legend does not mean fiction or fairy tale. Perhaps the best explanation of what legend is can be seen within the circle of the reader's own family background. Every family has its personal and private stories which are passed down from generation to generation by word of mouth. Invariably these stories are associated with this or that colorful or important relative. The reason for that association is not always clear, nor are the details of the stories. As a matter of fact, whatever details have been passed down have been embroidered and colored beyond all fact, or where details are lacking they have been fashioned either out of thin air or reasonable possibility. Whatever the case may be, these stories serve to preserve the memory and elucidate some aspect of the family's experience and past. So, for example, the stories of Moses' being hidden in a basket in the bullrushes and of David's conquest of Goliath and his great musical talent preserved the memory and elucidated aspects of the Hebrew nation's past and its relationship to God.

Myth, on the other hand, is a particular literary form, a kind of prose poetry in and through which an important thought or truth is dressed and communicated. Like legends, myths lend themselves easily to oral transmission, and the truths they embody are valid quite independently of the form in which they are dressed.

Take Ernest Hemingway's little classic, *The Old Man and the Sea*, as an example of what myth is and does. In this story Hemingway describes an old fisherman down on his luck. But one day the old fellow hooks a very large fish. After an exhausting struggle the old fellow reels the fish in and ties his catch to his small boat and heads for shore. The sharks, however, have other ideas. They swarm about the boat and despite the old man's efforts to drive them off, they feed upon the large fish until only the bones remain.

Now it is quite obvious that Hemingway could have summed up in just a few sentences what he had to say in this book. He could have written very simply—like a statistician making a report—that so and so many people believe that they are failures. But what would that have accomplished? Written as it was, Hemingway's story has helped many of its readers to rediscover themselves in the figure of that old fisherman. That is what myth does: it communicates truth in a way that people can see and recognize truth.

The Bible employs myth frequently and effectively. Take for example the story of the Fall in the book of Genesis. The author of this myth indicates quite clearly that the story he is relating is not about something that happened to an individual at the dawn of history. By giving his character the name Adam the author indicates that he is talking about the fate of all mankind, for in Hebrew the word we use as the name of Adam means mankind.

The point of this ancient myth is that everyone wants to rule his or her own life and resents any law—even divine law—that interferes with being one's own master. We prefer to make our own laws—laws which suit us. But what we want does not lead to the freedom we desire but to the bondage of guilt, and because we feel guilt our relationship to our fellow men is corrupted and defiled. Adam and Eve (which means womankind in Hebrew) concealed themselves from God behind bushes out of shame. And throughout the ages people have hidden and fled from God behind all kinds of bushes. In the final analysis the Eden stories of Genesis deal with man's sinful nature and attempts to attribute our own guilt to others, even to God himself. That is what human nature is like. Adam's problem of guilt is our problem as well.

The validity of the Bible's content, then, does not depend upon its literal truth and demonstrable authenticity. Rather, the validity of the Bible's content is established by the truth which is communicated to and recognized and grasped by the reader regardless of the literary form in which that truth is dressed.

Written for Flesh and Blood

It was said earlier in this book that the Bible complete from Genesis to Revelation did not fall from heaven into human hands. Rather, the Bible was written by a great many men over a long period of time. Moreover, what they wrote was written not out of a clear blue sky or inspired by the kind of thinking we associate with ivory towers. They wrote for people of flesh and blood, people involved in particular circumstances, people with particular problems and questions. The Bible's authors sought to address themselves to these circumstances, problems, and questions by using the kind of literary form and language that people understood. Thus, each book of the Bible has its own particular and unique literary form and style of language, its own special background.

Here are a few examples.

The author of the book of Jonah was faced with the problem of addressing himself to pious Jews who were very much concerned about the ritual niceties of religion, but who resented the idea that God could care about anyone but them. So the format he chose was one of humor and satire. He put his message in the form of a story about a godly Jew who tries to run away from what God calls him to do, is swallowed by a great fish (not a whale) and finally mourns for a decaying gourd instead of rejoicing at the salvation of the population of a non-Jewish city.

The Gospel of Matthew was written for Jews who had become Christians and saw Jesus in light of their Jewish background. The Gospel of Luke, on the other hand, was written by a Gentile Christian for fellow Gentiles.

The Book of Hebrews, which may have been written by a Jew, addressed itself to Jewish Christians in terms familiar to them.

The Epistle to the Colossians deals with one of the philosophies then current in Colossae and explains the gospel of Christ by using the terminology of the very philosophy the author sought to combat. By the same token the author of Ephesians used the language of religious enthusiasm which was well understood in that area. Thus, the flesh and blood people for whom the Bible was written had no difficulty in reading and understanding it.

The flesh-and-blood Bible reader of today, however, is often in the position of someone who finds and reads a letter written to an unknown person. To be sure, one can make some sense—perhaps even a great deal—out of what is read. But the full import of the letter is lost upon the reader who knows neither the

A palace relief depicting Hazael, king of Damascus (ca. 850 B.C.), bringing tribute to Shalmanezer III of Assyria.

writer, the addressee, nor the circumstances under which the letter was written. In order to become reasonably acquainted with the authors of the biblical books—especially those of the New Testament—and of the circumstances of those for and to whom they wrote, today's Bible reader will need some help. In Part Two some specific suggestions will be offered in this matter.

The Old Testament

For many who would like to read the Bible in a serious way, the Old Testament presents something of a problem. It is difficult at best to make any sense out of the conniving characteristic of so many Old Testament personalities. Even more perplexing and even distressing is what appears to us to be not only unethical but even immoral conduct on the part of even the best men and women we meet in the pages of the Old Testament. More often than not it is precisely things of this nature which impede the reader from discerning the message of the Old Testament. That message is important for the reader, for without a fairly clear picture of what that message is the New Testament is thoroughly incomprehensible.

In particular there are three Old Testament stumbling blocks about which the reader should be informed. One of them is the matter of polygamy, that is, the practice of having more than one wife at the same time, as was the case with Abraham and Jacob. To us such a practice is not only morally reprehensible but also forbidden by law. The Old Testament, however, had no such problem with this practice. In the Near Eastern world an unmarried or widowed woman was utterly without rights. Her only protection came from family ties. It was for this reason that when a man died (especially if he died without male descendants) his brother was responsible for caring for the widow, and, if necessary, for marrying and impregnating her so that his brother would have issue.

It was only after these social conditions had changed that Jesus spoke of monogamy as the will of God. At the same time we find Jesus befriending unmarried women. We assume that at least one of Jesus' female followers, Mary Magdalene, was unmarried, and that his own mother was a widow.

Another stumbling block to a reader of the Old Testament is the matter of animal sacrifice. Certainly the ritual slaughter and burning of animals is less repugnant than human sacrifice. Nonetheless, modern readers miss the point of such a practice. Actually such a practice bespeaks two things. One is man's desire to make an offering to God as an expression of gratitude. The other is to give tangible expression to man's desire to be reconciled to God, to be forgiven for his sin. In this case a man's sin was ritually transferred to an animal which then was slaughtered as a sign that the man's sins were dead.

The third stumbling block is circumcision. This is the minor surgical act by which male infants were initiated into the nation of God's chosen people, very much in the fashion in which a child is received into the Christian church by baptism. Circumcision is still practiced by Jews (and Muslims) as a religious rite and by others as a hygienic act.

The next three sections deal briefly with some information about the Old Testament which will shed light on the New Testament.

The Nature of Man and God's Steadfast Love

One thing the discerning person will note in reading the Old Testament is its kinship to much contemporary television programming. Both have sex and violence in common and abundance. The difference—and there certainly is a difference—lies however in the fact that the Old Testament does not deal with these themes in order to exploit the reader's prurient interests. The Old Testament speaks frankly (but not explicitly, as does much modern literature) and openly about incest, rape, and adultery. Nor does the Old Testament circumvent such grisly details of warfare as the running of threshers over women in advanced states of pregnancy or the decapitation of the corpses of defeated armies as tokens of victory. Treachery, perfidy, corruption in high places, political assassination, and common murder all play a role in the Old Testament's pages.

For a long time such things perplexed many readers—particularly those influenced by the prevalent idea that man is essentially good. The Old Testament labors under no such delusion. The Old Testament portrays man and his works as they really are: capable of much that is good, but at the same time inherently bent upon and capable of gross and heinous wickedness.

This is not the picture of man's nature we would like to have. But history, experience, and the behavioral sciences have shown us with distressing clarity how contradictory and complex man's nature is. That is exactly why the Old Testament treats such themes as those mentioned above: to illustrate what human nature is like. At the same time the Old Testament fortunately goes a step further. If the Old Testament stopped at simply giving us a portrait of human nature there could be no hope for man. The Old Testament says there is hope for man, a hope based not on man but on God. The Old Testament writers' experience of God convinced them that God would not abandon man despite all the evil of which human nature is capable and guilty.

Time and again the Old Testament tells us that although his people repeatedly betrayed and disobeyed him. God did not turn his back upon them. God was faithful to a faithless people. Though his love is spurned and rejected God continues to love his people. Thus, the Old Testament, in showing us the nature of man, also shows us the nature of God and anticipates the New Testament theme that God is love.

Social Concern

The biblical authors' perception and experience of God's steadfast and redemptive love for his people was also a perception and experience of man's need to respond to God's love. To the ancient commandment (Deut. 6:5) to love God with all one's heart, soul, and might they added, "and your neighbor as yourself." They realized in a very special way that to love God means to love one's neighbor in the sense of being actively concerned for the well-being of one's fellow man and for social justice. For this reason the pages of the Old Testament deal to a great extent with what we today call social issues.

Take for example the commandment to hallow the seventh day. For more reasons than can be enumerated here, this commandment is invariably understood in a cultic or ritualistic way. That is to say, this commandment has been associated almost exclusively with public worship and with abstention from work (and pleasure) for the sake of worship.

Actually this commandment can best be understood as an example of social concern. In the ancient Near Eastern world the wealthy did not work at all. The poor and slaves worked from dawn to dusk and knew no "day off." Israel, on the contrary, legislated a day of rest for man and beast to the glory of God to be sure, but to the well-being of men as well. When seen in this light, the commandment concerning the Sabbath is one of history's earliest pieces of social legislation.

A day of rest, of course, is not the only example of Old Testament concern with social questions and justice. The books of the prophets, for example, are brimming over with exhortations and calls to action in behalf of the oppressed, exploited, and deprived, and even absolute monarchs were not spared the scathing denunciation of the prophetic spokesmen for the Lord.

The discerning Bible reader will note that this passionate zeal of the Old Testament in social matters is absent from the New Testament. The reason for this is to be found in the early Christian expectation that the Lord was soon going to come again. In view of this overwhelming expectation early Christians did not deem it necessary to attempt to change the social order. The Lord would do that when he came. In addition to this preoccupation of early Christians with the Lord's coming again, there was another factor which accounts for their lack of social zeal. Christians constituted a tiny numerical minority in the world. Not only were their numbers small and insignificant; they were, with very rare exceptions, utterly without power or influence which would enable them to change anything.

Christians today are not, for the most part, preoccupied with the imminent end of the world and the Lord's "Second Coming" as they were two thousand years ago. Thus, not only can they hear with special sensitivity the Old Testament call to involvement in bringing about justice and change in the world, but also they are by virtue of their numbers and positions of power and influence able to effect the kind of social change envisaged by the prophets.

Much of what is seen in modern Israel is much the same as it was in biblical times. Bedouin tents have not changed very much over the past 3,000 years.

A view of the Lake of Gennesaret (opposite page, top); a typical Palestinian cistern in which rain water was gathered (opposite page, bottom); (above) looking out upon the Mediterranean Sea; (right) a eucalyptus tree.

A view of the lower Nile region (below) where the ancient Hebrews were held in bondage.

This handmill stands in front of the synagogue in Capernaum on the Lake of Gennesaret.

Wine and oil are kept in earthen vessels (opposite page, bottom).

A typical dwelling in Capernaum, similar to the one in which Jesus lived during his stay there.

Fishermen on the Lake of Gennesaret (opposite page, top); plowing with a wooden plow (right); the Negev Desert (opposite page, below); a typical cedar tree (below).

An olive tree (below) and a Near
Eastern vineyard (below, right).

Hope for the Future

One of the things which made the Jews so unique among the ancient peoples of the Mediterranean world was their view of history. Others thought of history as a repeating cycle with neither aim nor purpose nor goal. This view did not allow room for hope. What had been would be again and what is and was would always be. But that is not how the Jews interpreted history. The Old Testament saw both Israel and history as moving toward a goal. The seven days in the creation story of Genesis are a way of expressing this understanding of history. This concept of history enabled the Jews to look expectantly to the future, to look upon the future as a land of adventure.

The Jews could do this because of their experience of God. The outstanding event of Jewish history was the Exodus, when God led his people from slavery into freedom. After the initial excitement and thrill of their escape subsided, they became afraid. They knew what lay behind them. Bad as that was, they were even more frightened and apprehensive of what lay ahead of them in the wilderness of Palestine. Yet, to their amazement, God was there ahead of them. When they crossed the Jordan River into the "promised land" they were afraid that God would desert them. Their fears were groundless. He did not abandon them then, nor did he abandon them when they were carried off into captivity in Babylonia. He was with them even there on the banks of the Tigris and Euphrates as they met together in synagogs and gathered and put to paper the traditions and writings which make up much of the Old Testament.

In one way or another the Old Testament has the ring of a national confession of faith which says, in effect: "Time and again we stood with fear at the door of the future, and time and again God put us to shame by opening the door of the future to us." For Israel God was not to be reckoned with only in the past; the future as well is in his hand. Nothing was more certain for the Old Testament prophets than the expectation that God would remain true to form and continue to astonish his people with his works in the future as he had in the past. So Isaiah, for example (see especially chapters 4 and 11), could look forward to a realm and era of peace. It was in expectation of that era to which the prophets had pointed that Jesus lived, and what he said about the kingdom of God being at hand can be understood only in light of the Old Testament's confidence concerning the future.

The New Testament—A Book of Confidence

The conviction which underlies the New Testament is that the Old Testament vision is not a utopian dream but a coming reality which is being realized here and now. That reality began with the coming of Jesus Christ. This conviction can be likened to that of prisoners of war who, though still huddled within their compounds and surrounded by barbed wire, know that the war has ended and that in effect they are already on their way home.

In part this New Testament conviction rests upon the Old Testament understanding of history as moving toward a God-appointed goal. For the most part, however, the New Testament conviction derives from the Christian experience of Jesus Christ's lordship over the cosmos. Like their Old Testament predecessors, the New Testament writers look to the future with neither dread nor human optimism, but with confidence in him who promised, "Behold, I have set before you an open door . . ." (Rev. 7:8).

The Foretaste of Freedom

The word *escapist* is used to describe a person who pays no heed to the present but instead dwells upon and fantasizes about the future. Such behavior is essentially neurotic. But there is a great difference between such neuroticism and the confidence and faith with which the New Testament writers looked to the future. That difference is summed up in the person of Jesus Christ, who, the New Testament writers declared, not only proclaimed the future, but actually gave men a foretaste of the future that is to be.

Let us look at a particular example of that foretaste: freedom from guilt.

The New Testament writers recognized that guilt is something very real. Men cannot simply shrug it off as though it were nothing. They carry their guilt with them wherever they go, into whatever they do. To a degree men can and do manage to live comfortably with their guilt—at least with some forms of guilt. They have learned that guilt can be sublimated or disguised. Yet guilt always asserts itself in one way or another. One of these ways is the sorrow for what one is and had done which the Bible calls repentance. He who experiences and recognizes this sorrow for what it is is prepared to receive the forgiveness that Christ offers. It is this forgiveness which sets us free from the haunting, disabling memory of what we ourselves cannot change, and empowers us to make a new start in life. In effect, this forgiveness means that we are set free from the past to begin a new life, a new way of life, not someday in the far distant future, but here and now, today. This is what the New Testament means when it speaks of a new birth and of a new creation. Thus, the New Testament is saying that through the forgiveness of Jesus Christ the burden of the past has been lifted, that today is no longer overshadowed by the guilt of yesterday and the threat of tomorrow. For the Christian life, true life, begins with a forgiveness that changes today and tomorrow.

Freedom from Laws and Rules

It was stated earlier in this book that the New Testament writers, because of their belief that Jesus would soon return,

An oven and pitcher used in Jesus' day.

רוּחַ אֲדֹנָי יְהוִה עָלָי יַעַן מָשַׁח יְהוָה אֹתִי
לְבַשֵּׂר עֲנָוִים שְׁלָחַנִי לַחֲבֹשׁ לְנִשְׁבְּרֵי־לֵב
לִקְרֹא לִשְׁבוּיִם דְּרוֹר וְלַאֲסוּרִים פְּקַח־קוֹחַ:
לִקְרֹא שְׁנַת־רָצוֹן לַיהוָה וְיוֹם נָקָם לֵאלֹהֵינוּ
לְנַחֵם כָּל־אֲבֵלִים:

The Old Testament was written in the Hebrew language. The passage
shown above is the Hebrew verse which Jesus read and commented
on in his first sermon in the synagog at Nazareth (Is. 61:1, 2;
see Luke 4:16–21). NOTE: Hebrew is read from right to left.

πνεῦμα κυρίου ἐπ' ἐμέ, οὗ εἵνεκεν ἔχρισέν με
εὐαγγελίσασθαι πτωχοῖς, ἀπέσταλκέν με.
κηρῦξαι αἰχμαλώτοις ἄφεσιν καὶ τυφλοῖς ἀνάβλε-
ἀποστεῖλαι τεθραυσμένους ἐν ἀφέσει,   [ψιν,
κηρῦξαι ἐνιαυτὸν κυρίου δεκτόν.

The New Testament was written in the Greek language, which was
the most commonly understood language of the Mediterranean world
of Jesus' day. The passage shown above is the same passage shown
in Hebrew on the opposite page (Is. 61:1, 2) as it is quoted in the
Greek text of Luke 4:18–19.

Spiritus Domini super me propter
  quod unxit me
evangelizare pauperibus misit me
praedicare captivis remissionem et
  caecis visum
dimittere confractos in remissionem
praedicare annum Domini acceptum
  et diem retributionis

Luke 4:18–19 is shown above in the Latin or Vulgate translation
dating from 382 A.D. The Vulgate translation is the official Latin
New Testament text of the Roman Catholic Church.

showed none of the social zeal that is found in the Old Testament, particularly in the prophets. The Bible reader will note
yet another striking difference between the Old and New Testaments: the absence of moral legislation, specific, detailed rules
for personal conduct. The reason for this can perhaps be best
illustrated against the background of the Sabbath. At the outset,
the institution of the Sabbath was humanitarian, the intention
being to guarantee a day of rest for man and beast. For a long
time the Sabbath was observed for precisely that reason. But in
the course of time that original purpose was increasingly sub-
merged under an ocean of ritual laws and observances to a point
that the original intent and purpose of the Sabbath was for-
gotten. In Jesus' day there were some 170 laws governing the
Sabbath. For example, it was forbidden: to eat an egg laid on the
Sabbath; to put a cast on a broken arm or leg (at best it was
permitted to relieve the pain by pouring cold water on the in-
jured limb); to perform any kind of medical act.

Jesus paid no attention to such rules and regulations. He healed on the Sabbath because to him helping people who needed help was far more important than ritual observances and ceremonial niceties. In this, as in other matters, Jesus was, in effect, laying down a fundamental standard on which all Christian conduct is based: the law of love, of concern for the well-being of one's neighbor. For Christians that is the standard of conduct which conforms to Christ's love for men. Christians in New Testament times did not always practice such a high morality. Often they accepted uncritically the old regulations, even those which were inhumane and often patently foolish. Thus, the New Testament freedom from laws and rules is not an abolition of standards of conduct but the establishment of a more demanding, more godly, more humane standard of conduct. Instead of drawing up rules and regulations, the New Testament provides a basic approach by which Christians in every generation deal with questions of ethical and moral decision.

The Cross of Christ

As we have seen, there was a great religious gap between the Jews and their Gentile neighbors. The God of Israel could not be reduced to man's level; he could not be imprisoned in nature or in any idol or edifice. For Israel God is above and beyond man. Nor did the New Testament retreat from the Old Testament position. In fact, the New Testament goes even further and affirms that the God who is free of man made unexpected use of his freedom by revealing himself in Jesus of Nazareth. Such an affirmation was inconceivable even to those who shared most strongly the Old Testament understanding of God. Even more, such an affirmation was an offense, a scandal, to the Jews because Jesus was put to death on the cross.

If, however, the Christian affirmation that God was incarnate in the crucified Jesus Christ was a scandal and a blasphemy to the Jews, it was sheer nonsense to the Greeks. If there is a God, the Greeks said, then it was inconceivable to them that at some accidental point in time he would choose to appear in flesh and blood in the person of an itinerant preacher in a politically insignificant nation. If God does in fact reveal himself, the

Greeks argued, then he does so through a system of logical thought which is valid for all times.

The New Testament, however, does not try to overcome either the Jewish or the Greek criticism of the Christian affirmation with arguments or proofs. Rather, the New Testament bears witness to the God who is infinitely greater than the power attributed to him by the Jews or the logical consistency demanded of deity by the Greeks. What the New Testament affirms and confesses is that in Jesus Christ and his death on the cross God takes his place at the side of suffering mankind. That is what the cross of Christ is all about. God does not help and redeem man by displays of raw power or through logical explanations of the mysteries and perplexities of life. He helps and redeems men and women by coming down and sharing and overcoming what Paul called the last enemy, Death itself.

Security and a Meaningful Life

How can we find security and lead a meaningful life? This question is by no means peculiar to our day and age. In many ways men have always asked this question. This is one of the major questions with which the Bible deals. In fact, Saint Paul devoted the entire Epistle to the Romans to this question. Paul's answer to the age-old question "What must I do?" is that one finds security and a meaningful life only when something else precedes our human efforts to achieve what we so earnestly seek.

That "something else" can be illustrated from what we observe and know about the development of a child. The way a child develops depends upon how he or she is accepted. Where a child finds acceptance, there the child finds security. In Romans Paul makes it clear that through faith in Jesus Christ we realize that God accepts us without regard to what we have done or achieved. In short, we do not earn what we seek (salvation is one of the words we use to describe what we seek), it is ours when we realize that through Jesus Christ God accepts us as we are. He does not demand proof of our good intentions or evidences of accomplishment. He gives us himself, and in trusting him we find the security we crave.

To be sure, such a message can be misunderstood and perverted. Some would and indeed have taken it to mean that

what one does is of no matter, that one can do as one pleases. Others would and have taken this to mean that all that matters is for one to cultivate one's own inner life and to be oblivious of everything else. But that is not what Paul is saying in Romans. Paul is saying that he who knows that he is accepted and loved by God is freed from anxiety in order to lead a meaningful life, to do the things that are really important and necessary. That is why Paul calls the gospel "the power of God to salvation," and why Luther spoke of faith and trust in God as something that is living, active, and busy. The person who knows he or she is accepted and loved by God is at the same time led to see what it is to which one's mind and physical energies can be applied in a way that fulfills God's will. In all honesty it must be said that what we are led to see is rarely spectacular or earth-shaking; more often it is quite ordinary and plain. Yet this is precisely what it is that makes life meaningful.

Spiritual and Spirit

The writers of the Bible were creatures of their times. Like their contemporaries, they believed that the universe was a four-story affair. At the top was heaven, the dwelling-place of God and the habitat of angels. Between heaven and earth was the realm of the spirits. Earth was the dwelling-place of man, and at the bottom of the universe was the realm of the dead.

This view of the universe, of course, is no longer acceptable. Because this view is no longer acceptable some theologians have taken the position that there is only one kind of reality, namely, the one we can see and investigate by scientific methods. Some of these theologians have gone so far as to remove the words *spiritual* and *spirit* from the religious vocabulary. Strange to say, however, many modern scientists whom we would expect to agree with such theologians take the opposite position. Many of these scientists are more cautious and reverent when it comes to what we call spiritual things. For them the universe, despite our expanding knowledge of it, becomes more and more perplexing and mysterious.

The Bible does not shy away from what we call the spiritual and spirit. This does not mean that when the Bible treats such matters it is affirming the parallel existence of another kind of

Cultic vessels in the shape of animals.

material world to which our fleshly eyes are blind. Rather, the Bible is trying to describe the ways in which the divine works upon and in the world in which we live. The words *spiritual* and *spirit* may not be the most precise and exact terms, but they serve to communicate and describe what the Bible is talking about.

Obviously neither the Bible nor anything nor anyone else can classify and catalog exhaustively the ways in which God works. Instead, the Bible speaks of the works of the Spirit, and by this means the working of God in everything that proceeds from the relationship of man to God through Jesus Christ. One of the most important acts of God which the Bible describes as a work of the Spirit is when our whole life is so radically changed that our outlook, thinking, and action undergo a complete turn-about, and our life's horizons and dimensions are widened, broadened, and deepened. Here again the Bible reader must be alert to reading the Bible for the truth it communicates and not be distracted by the ways and words it uses as vehicles of communication.

PART TWO

How
to
Read
the
Bible

Which Translation Shall I Use?

There was a time when the question "Which translation shall I use?" would never have occurred to English-speaking Christians. Protestants had the King James Version of the Bible, so-called because this translation was commissioned by James I, Protestant king of England, and completed in 1611. Catholics, on the other hand, had the Douay Bible, which derived its name from a town in France where Roman Catholic refugees from James's England produced their own English translation.

In the three-and-a-half centuries since then (especially in the last half-century), there have been a great many English translations and paraphrases of the Bible. The King James and Douay translations are still widely used. (In fact, the King James Version has left an irradicable mark upon the English language.) But more and more Bible readers are turning to such contemporary translations as the *Revised Standard Version, The Jerusalem Bible, The New English Bible.* The ecumenical *Common Bible,* published in 1973 under Roman Catholic and Protestant auspices, is not a new translation but an edition of the *Revised Standard Version* that has been expanded to include the Apocryphal books and can be used by Catholics and Protestants alike. Any of the versions mentioned here (and others as well) can be commended to the serious Bible reader. These versions have been prepared by teams of recognized, qualified, and responsible scholars on the basis of the most reliable sources in the original languages.

Which of these versions or translations is the best? Obviously that one is best which the reader finds the most comfortable to read, the language of which speaks most readily and effectively to the reader. In short, that translation is best which speaks the most understandable English to the English-speaking reader.

Ways to Read the Bible

1. FROM COVER TO COVER

It is said that George Ansbach, a contemporary of Martin Luther, read the Bible from cover to cover some fifty-eight times during his life. That must be some kind of a world record. It has been estimated that it would take about five-hundred hours to read the Bible in this way. Reading at the rate of a chapter a day, one could read through the Bible in three years and ninety-four days.

But to be quite honest, to read the Bible page for page, from one cover to another can be a tedious and unrewarding business. The reader can become quite bored and lose all enthusiasm because, frankly speaking, many passages are boring, monotonous, and difficult. For example, many of the laws and regulations deal with matters utterly alien to our experience. Nor are we interested in or edified by genealogies and the like. Moreover, the books of 1 and 2 Chronicles repeat much of what is related in much livelier style in 1 and 2 Samuel and 1 and 2 Kings.

The 260 chapters of the New Testament can be read more quickly, easily, and profitably than the Old Testament. Should the reader choose to read the New Testament first, it would be advisable first to lay hold of a general introduction to the New Testament and to become familiar with the setting and theme of a book before reading it. Many Bibles have just such an introduction either at the beginning of each book or in an appendix, along with tables and explanations of coins, weights, and measures mentioned in the Bible and the maps which help the reader to visualize the location of the places which play an important role in the biblical narrative.

2. SELECTED PASSAGES

A far better and more profitable way to read the Bible is to read short, selected passages. This can be done in a number of ways:

a. A single book at a time. In choosing which book to read one should follow one's personal inclination, expectation, curiosity, or personal need. More will be said of this below.

b. One can follow the reading plan published each year by the American Bible Society, of a favorite devotional publication, or the daily Bible readings suggested by various denominations and many congregations.

c. Certain denominations (e.g., Lutheran, Episcopal, Methodist, Roman Catholic, Presbyterian, Disciples of Christ, United Church of Christ) have a fixed series of Scripture lessons which are read in the services each Sunday. Usually the sermon is based on one of these lessons. By reading these lessons before the Sunday services the sermon and Scripture readings will be more meaningful to the worshiper.

3. SOMETHING TO SUIT ONE'S MOOD

Is that really possible? After all, each of us has many moods. Today we are in the mood for a detective story; tomorrow for poetry; another day, social critique or adventure or something philosophical.

The Bible is a miniature library; it has something for every literary mood and taste. The only problem is to match the mood with the appropriate passage or book. Here are a few suggestions:

a. Excitement and Adventure

Abraham the Wanderer: Genesis 12; 13; 15—25:8.

Joseph—pampered scion who rose from slavery to a viceroy's throne: Genesis 37:2–35; 39—50.

The Birth of a Nation: Exodus.

Carving Out a Homeland: Numbers.

Gideon the Warrior: Judges 6—8.

Samson the Strong Man: Judges 13—16.

David: Shepherd, Outlaw, King: 1 Samuel 16—20; 23:14—25:42; 27:1-3; 31; 2 Samuel 5—7; 11—13; 15; 16; 18—19:9; 21:15—23:7; 1 Kings 1—2:12.

A Reluctant Prophet: The Book of Jonah.

On the Missionary Trail: Acts 13:1—14:28; 15:36—25:22; 27:1—28:30.

b. Passages for Reflection

In recent years meditation has become quite fashionable. It is not difficult to see why. With increasing frequency more and more people are becoming persuaded that there is—or should be—more to life than the "rat race"; that there is—or should be—more to life than meets the eye. Meditation and reflection offer a way of probing life's depth and meaning.

Nor are meditation and reflection as difficult as some people think. If one receives a letter which brings joyful or disturbing news, one thinks about that news for hours, days, weeks. That is what meditation and reflection are, and there is much in the Bible which invites, even demands, meditation and reflection. The following are such passages:

Jesus' Parables: Matthew 13:1-9, 18-23, 24-30, 44-46; 20:1-16; 25:31-46; Luke 10:25-37; 14:15-24; 15:1-32; 18:1-14; 19:11-27.

Individual Verses: John 8:12; 10:7-9; 10:11-15; 11:25-26; 14:6; 15:1-5; 18:37.

Some have found it helpful to make note of passages they have found perplexing and have gone back to reflect and meditate upon them. The result is that often upon reflection and meditation what was obscure becomes clear and what was confusing becomes a helpful insight.

c. Poetry

The Bible contains some of the greatest poetry ever written. Try these as a sample: Song of Solomon; Job (especially chapters 1—14; 29—30; 32—33; 38—42); 1 Corinthians 13; Romans 8:31-39; Philippians 2:5-11; Luke 1:46-55.

The poetic treasure chest of the Bible, however, is the book of Psalms. Here one finds no pious drivel. Here men and women of real flesh and blood and feeling speak of the things that are

The people of the modern Near East still look very much like those of Jesus' day.

really on their minds and hearts. They lament and rejoice; they ponder and despair; they give voice both to the darkest despair and torturous inner conflict and to the most exhilarating heights of hope and faith and inner peace. Here we find the articulation of our deepest feelings. To read them aloud (especially Psalms 18, 22, 23, 42, 51, 73, 90, 103, 126, 139) is to discover that praying is not such a strange exercise after all, for despite their beauty and rhythm the psalms are prayers, the kind of prayers that all of us can and at times do pray.

Next to the Book of Psalms the Book of Job is probably the greatest piece of biblical poetry. The poem tells the story of how a good and decent man tries to make sense out of the misfortunes that befall him. The reader finds himself caught up with Job as he struggles with the same issues and problems and questions with which we struggle. We hear all of the old clichés and superficial explanations as we, with Job, wrestle with God for the wisdom born of faith and trust.

d. Biography

The Bible contains a great many biographical and autobiographical passages. We learn a great deal of personal information about the great Old Testament prophet Jeremiah in passages such as Jeremiah 1:1–3; 4:19–31; 6:1—7:15; 9; 11:18—13:14; 15:10—16:13; 17:14–18; 19—20; 23:1–8; 26; 28; 31—32; 36—40; 42—43.

The great apostle Paul relates numerous incidents in his life and we find much first-hand biographical and personal information about him in his letters, particularly in 1 and 2 Corinthians, Galatians, Philippians, and 1 Thessalonians. In addition to biographical material we also see in Paul's letters how he dealt with a wide variety of theological, institutional, and moral questions in an age when such matters had to be dealt with in writing and at a distance.

e. Theology

Not everyone is always interested in adventure or biography or poetry. There are times when we need and want to dig into something that gives us a clear and incisive presentation of Christian faith and teaching. This, too, can be found in the Bible. Paul's Epistle to the Romans is a classic exposition and summary of the Christian faith. Here Paul expounds the guilt of believer and nonbeliever alike and of God's redemptive work for both (chapters 1–3). Here, too, Paul deals with baptism and the Holy Spirit (6; 7:7–25; 8:12–39); the future of the Jews (chapter 11); the Christian life in a non-Christian environment; the believer and the state; and the Christian's hope. This Epistle to the Romans is an immensely rewarding piece of biblical literature, but it is not easy reading, and the reader should keep a commentary or some other help at hand when reading this epistle.

f. Practical Guides to Living

Just as there is more to life than the daily grind in which all of us are caught up, so there is much truth and insight into life and its problems which is not complex in thought or application. We find such practical wisdom and experience embodied in the Old Testament books of Proverbs and Ecclesiastes. Of course, one cannot always apply literally what one reads there. The times have wrought many changes in the relationship between parents and children, husbands and wives, employers and employees. Nonetheless, these books provoke a great deal of thought and offer many an insight to us in our day.

Where to Look for Help

Regardless of the translation or version one chooses, there are going to be times when the Bible speaks as clearly, directly, and familiarly as an old and trusted friend. There will be no doubt in the reader's mind as to what the Bible says and means. But there will be times when certain passages, perhaps whole chapters and even entire books, will be a total mystery to the reader. Quite frankly, this cannot be avoided. In fact, it would be a strange state of affairs if one were to read the Bible without being confused (sometimes even bored), being uncertain of what one is reading, or without having certain questions come into mind to which one finds no answer. What does one do in such a case?

Obviously, one should seek help. After all, the Bible was not written in incomprehensible tongues which only charismatics can interpret. The Bible was written in languages spoken and understood by real people and was meant to be understood by all, not by just a few. Moreover, as has been pointed out earlier in this book, the various books of the Bible were written over a long period of time and under a variety of historical circumstances. In order to understand these writings most fully, the Bible reader should be as familiar as possible with the circumstances under which the various books were written, who the various people were whom one encounters in the biblical text, what the events were which are mentioned or alluded to. Briefly stated, the Bible reader needs to know the "who, what, where, when, and why" of the various books of the Bible.

It is for this reason that commentaries on and introductions to the Bible are written and published. The majority of these commentaries and introductions are written for clergymen and for the most part are too technical and detailed for the average layman. There are, however, commentaries and introductions which are written and published especially for laymen. These commentaries and introductions are written by competent, able scholars and teachers who seek to answer the basic questions of "who, what, where, when, and why" without all of the details and mechanics which only trained theologians can use. Public and congregational libraries usually have such books. Secular as well as church publishing houses issue commentaries and introductions, and these are advertised in their catalogs which are usually available in bookstores.

One will not find all the answers to one's questions in books, however adequate and excellent those books may be. Nor should one expect to find all the answers in a book. The Bible deals with the interpretation of life and reality, not with hard and fixed facts to which the answers never change or vary and can be listed and cataloged in print.

Yet there are two avenues open to the Bible reader seeking answers to questions which arise from reading Scripture. One avenue is to discuss one's questions with a trained and trustworthy clergyman with whom one feels comfortable and at ease. The other avenue is to take part in group Bible studies. There, one has the benefit of the insights and experiences of others who are pursuing the same goal. In the act of sharing insight and experience one thing is certain: the printed word of the Bible becomes the living word of God. It is through that living word that the God who spoke to and through the patriarchs, prophets, and apostles in the past now speaks to us in the present.

The world has changed greatly since the time the Bible was written. What has not changed, however, is the human quest for the meaning of life and for a hope which is not an illusion.

PART THREE

The Bible's Books in Summary

The Old Testament

GENESIS. The book of beginnings! Here the reader finds the majestic creation stories and the story of mankind's beginning under the figures of Adam and Eve. The origins of the Hebrew people are recounted and narrated in the stories of Abraham, Isaac, Jacob and his twelve sons, and the Hebrew settlement in Egypt under the sponsorship of Joseph.

EXODUS. Many years had passed since the days of Joseph's prominence in Egypt. The Hebrews were now subjected to oppression and persecution. Under the leadership of Moses this people experiences the power and mercy of God in unique ways, and through the giving of the Ten Commandments the Hebrews become God's chosen people. Delivered from oppression in Egypt, the Hebrews become a nomadic people in search of a "promised land."

LEVITICUS. Taking its name from the tribe of Levi, from which Israel's priests came, this book sets forth in considerable detail the worship and moral practices of the Jewish nation. The reader will marvel that there is not a single area of life untouched by the relationship between God and man.

NUMBERS. Here the story begun in Exodus is picked up and carried forth as the Hebrews continue their nomadic existence but begin to fix their eyes on Canaan as the promised land and make their plans accordingly.

DEUTERONOMY. Meaning "second law," this book is a review of the nation's divine calling and history from the pen of devout and godly men far removed in time from the events of which they tell. The intent of the book is to remind a people long settled in the promised land of their past struggles and of God's faithfulness.

JOSHUA. Though Moses had led his people out of Egypt, he would not be able to lead them into the promised land. Following Moses' death, leadership fell to Joshua. Under Joshua the Hebrew "pioneers" fought their way in a series of battles into the "promised land" which was partitioned among the twelve tribes.

JUDGES. Like the pioneers of the American West, the Hebrews had homes to build, farms to cultivate, and families to rear. From time to time hostile native tribes sought to drive out the newcomers. In times of danger men called Judges (among them: Gideon, Jephtha, and Samson) assumed military leadership.

RUTH. The beautiful story of a Moabite girl and her loyalty to the mother of her deceased husband.

1 AND 2 SAMUEL. Samuel the prophet (spokesman for God) was the last of the Judges. Yielding to the will of the people for a king, Samuel anointed Saul as Israel's first king. The two books of Samuel tell the story of Israel and its climb to power and greatness under its first two kings, Saul and David. But in both books we see as well the weaknesses of great and powerful men and the consequences for a nation.

1 AND 2 KINGS AND 1 AND 2 CHRONICLES. In all four books the reader follows the events of some forty successors of King David. Kings and Chronicles tell much the same story, although from different perspectives. The story they tell relates what led up to the division, fall, and exile of the nation and its people. Chronicles carries the story a bit further than Kings when it

reports the return of the Jews to their homeland after an exile of seventy years in Babylonia.

EZRA. The story of the return of the exiles and of the rebuilding of the Temple. The second half of the book deals with the work of Ezra in reforming the religious practices of the new generation of returnees.

NEHEMIAH. The story of a man who gave up an important position in the court of the King of Persia to help the returned exiles to secure the defenseless city of Jerusalem against the attacks of brigands.

ESTHER. Not all of the Jews chose to return to their homeland. Many remained where they were at various locations in the Persian empire and often became objects of hatred and oppression. This book tells the story of how a Jewish girl who had become Queen of Persia saved these Jews from extinction.

JOB. Life had been good to Job and his large family. Then, suddenly, everything fell apart for him. Death, illness, financial loss, and mental depression plagued Job all the way. "Why," the book asks, "does a good man suffer?" The answer Job discovered lies not in an explanation but in an understanding of life that defies arguments and explanations.

PSALMS. Actually a collection of five books of poetry, the Book of Psalms lays bare the hearts of God-fearing men and women as they react to the joys, sorrows, and trials of life and pour out their hearts to God in song and prayer.

PROVERBS. Here the reader will find, often in brief, pithy form, a collection of sayings and observations based on very practical experience and dealing with such matters as the training of children, control of the tongue, laziness, the use of money, married life, etc.

ECCLESIASTES. "Why do we live; what is the meaning of life?" The Preacher (the title used by the author of this book) looked at all the answers people gave then (and still give today) and concluded that without God life has neither meaning nor sense.

SONG OF SOLOMON. Although it is sometimes difficult to say who is speaking when, this book is a kind of romantic play. Tradition has it that the hero was Solomon and the heroine a girl he planned to marry. The book expresses the deep love the couple had for each other.

ISAIAH. The first thirty-nine chapters of this book preserve the message of a prophet to a nation that did not want to hear the truth about its morals and policies. The rest of the book contains a message of redemption so startling and different in outlook that the Christian church has regarded Isaiah's characterization of a suffering servant as the depiction of the suffering Christ.

JEREMIAH. It is never an easy task to speak the truth—especially when the truth is distasteful to those who must hear it. Yet that is precisely the task to which Jeremiah was called. Despite attempts on his life to silence him, Jeremiah was faithful to his task. Eventually the danger of which he had warned came to pass. Even though Jeremiah was regarded as a traitor by many, he was able to hold out hope to his people.

LAMENTATIONS. "You never miss the water till the well runs dry" is an axiom of life not just a much-quoted saying. After the fall of Jerusalem and the carrying of thousands of Israelites into captivity, Jeremiah's people brooded over what they had lost and lamented what they had done to bring about such a state of affairs. In their lamentation the Israelites perceived the great truth that suffering, misfortune, and even punishment at the hand of God serve a useful and divine purpose.

EZEKIEL. There were Israelites who refused to see their nation's defeat and their condition as exiles as the consequence of their own sin. Bitterly and unrealistically these exiles complained that God was punishing them for the sins of their parents and grandparents. Ezekiel's task was to help these people to see their own responsibility for what had befallen them. In helping his people to understand and acknowledge their own very real guilt, Ezekiel enabled his people to look to the future with hope and determination.

DANIEL. The lot of the Israelite captives in exile was by no means all bad. Many of them became quite successful, particularly in business and often in government service. The Book of Daniel is the story of one such Israelite who, though it often involved considerable risk, insisted upon retaining his ethnic identity and faith in God in a foreign and hostile environment.

HOSEA. Hosea loved his wife Gomer very deeply, but his love meant little to her. She was faithless to him and finally ran off to live with one of her lovers, who soon tired of her and sold her into slavery. But Hosea, regardless of his wife's past and what others thought, still loved her and bought her out of slavery and took her into his home. In that shattered and restored relationship of love Hosea saw the story of his people's relationship to God. Although this is one of the shorter books of the Bible, Hosea is one of the most deeply moving of its stories.

JOEL. For farmers in the Bible lands a plague of locusts was one of the worst things that could happen. These creatures ate every growing plant and left hunger and famine in their wake. It was just such a plague that Joel foretold as a picture of the wrath of God upon the sins of the people. But like other prophets before and after him, Joel foresaw the day when the spirit of God would be poured out on the people in such a measure that all the enemies of God would be overcome.

AMOS. Here was a prophet who exposed and excoriated the sins of an affluent and hypocritical society with a passion and eloquence undiminished by the passing of the centuries. Amos's God was not only a God of personal piety but a God of social justice as well.

OBADIAH. One of the nations which had helped to pave the way for the downfall of Jerusalem was Edom, whose people were related to the Israelites (the Edomites were descendants of Esau). Obadiah denounced their perfidy and declared that the day would come when this nation, despite its mountain strongholds, would be punished for its betrayal of blood, kin, and neighbors.

JONAH. Jonah was so determined not to obey God's call to preach to the people of Nineveh that he took to the sea to escape God. In this humorous little book we see how God overcomes the bigotry, prejudice, and disobedience of his prophet to work his will and way.

MICAH. When the worst is behind us and things are going better, we quickly forget all the vows and promises we made to God and others that we would change our ways. After their return from exiles the Jews did that very thing. They cheated

God and each other—just as they had done before the exile. And like the prophets before him, Micah exposed the empty formal religion used to cover the people's hypocrisy and pointed to a coming savior.

NAHUM. Some 600 years before Christ, Assyria was the most powerful nation in the world. At that very time Nahum foretold that God would overthrow that nation because of its greed and its ruthlessness. God, Nahum said, would punish such wickedness. Not many years later, that which seemed impossible came to pass, and three centuries later not a trace of Assyria's capital could be found.

HABAKKUK. There are times when even the most faithful person wonders if God knows what he is doing. Habakkuk was one of these people. He knew that his nation had sinned and deserved punishment. What he could not understand was why God would use an even more sinful, wicked nation as the rod of his punishment. The pursuit of this question is the theme of Habakkuk's prophecy.

ZEPHANIAH. When Josiah came to the throne of Judah he was only a boy. Under the long reign of his predecessor many of the people had turned to worshiping the stars and even practiced human sacrifice. Under the influence of Zephaniah's preaching, Josiah reformed the nation and the prophet saw what very few prophets ever see: the successful fruit of their labors.

HAGGAI. When the Jews returned from exile in 538 B.C. they vowed to rebuild the Temple of the Lord. As is often the case with such vows and intentions, the people put other things first, with the result that nothing they did really succeeded. Haggai's message was that the people should do what they had promised, and that having put God where he belongs in their lives (in first place) everything else would fall into place.

ZECHARIAH. A contemporary of Haggai, Zechariah's prophetic work consisted largely of encouraging the Jews at the work of rebuilding the Temple. The last part of the book contains a look to the future and the promised Savior.

MALACHI. Despite their long history which demonstrated God's love and will for them, the returned Jewish exiles began to doubt that God really cared about them. They became apathetic and careless in their worship and through increasing intermarriage with the unbelievers of surrounding tribes and nations, they were in danger of losing what remained of their identity and faith. It was Malachi who exhorted the people to hold fast, for the day of the promised Savior was not far off. His coming would mean salvation and triumph for God and his people.

The Apocrypha/Deuterocanonical Books

The term Apocrypha/Deuterocanonical is applied to the following books usually dispersed throughout the Old Testament in Roman Catholic Bibles and grouped together between the Old and New Testaments in some Protestant editions of the Bible: Tobit, Judith, Esther, Wisdom of Solomon, Ecclesiasticus or the Wisdom of Jesus the Son of Sirach, Baruch, The Letter of Jeremiah, The Prayer of Azariah and the Song of the Three Young Men, Susanna, Bel and the Dragon, The First Book of Maccabees, The Second Book of Maccabees, First Esdras, Second Esdras, The Prayer of Manasseh.

Catholics and Protestants disagree as to the authority these books have for Christians. With the exception of First and Second Esdras and the Prayer of Manasseh, Catholics accept these books as canonical (authoritative) Scripture. Protestants generally regard them as useful and edifying reading matter.

The New Testament

The first four books of the New Testament bear the title *Gospels* because they tell (each in its own way) of the life, message, death, and resurrection of Jesus Christ.

MATTHEW devotes much of his Gospel to Jesus' teaching and appears to direct his book to early Jewish Christians.

MARK is believed by many to be the oldest of the four Gospels. This Gospel emphasizes not so much what Jesus said as what he did; consequently Mark reports a great many miracles and healings.

LUKE wrote his Gospel in the form of a letter to a man named Theophilus, to whom Luke was seeking to tell the story of Jesus from the very beginning. Although Luke relates much of the same material given by Matthew and Mark, he also includes much material (particularly parables) that is unique to his Gospel.

JOHN is quite different from the other Gospels in a number of ways, and for that reason it makes especially interesting reading. John's intention was not to relate the whole life and work of Jesus but rather to concentrate on a few incidents in the Lord's life and in such a way as to persuade the reader that Jesus is indeed the Savior of the world.

The Book of ACTS was probably written as a part of Luke's Gospel. Here is told the story of the birth and outreach of the Christian church from the frightened band of believers in Jerusalem to Paul's preparation to appear before the emperor of Rome. This book recounts the missionary work of Peter and especially of Paul as they and countless individuals encountered here take the gospel to the corners of the earth.

The term *Epistles* is applied to the following books because they were originally letters of a kind, sometimes personal or general letters, or letters in the form of tracts addressed to no one person or group in particular but to any or all in general.

ROMANS is a highly theological letter in which Paul sets forth the Christian faith as he teaches it to the Christian believers in Rome.

1 AND 2 CORINTHIANS are letters written by Paul to a congregation in a large and worldly city. This congregation was beset by a host of practical and personal problems of faith and morals which persist to this day, and Paul's letters are the great apostle's advice and guidance in dealing with these problems.

GALATIANS is one of the earliest New Testament Epistles. Many Christians were of the opinion that in order to become Christians, Gentiles first had to become Jews and observe Jewish law. Here Paul deals with this question and the larger question of grace and faith over against law and works.

EPHESIANS deals largely with the question of what the church is and what Christians are. Here Paul gives trustworthy advice concerning the relationships of husbands and wives, children and parents, masters (employers) and slaves (employees).

PHILIPPIANS was written to a congregation which had a very special place in Paul's heart. This is a very friendly letter in which Paul, writing from prison, thanks the brethren in Philippi for their remembrance of him and encourages their faith and works.

COLOSSIANS. Paul had never been to Colossae. The congregation there had been founded by others. Certain teachers had invaded the congregation who had introduced false and superstitious teachings. Paul wrote to emphasize that salvation is through Jesus Christ, not angels, feasts, or holy days.

1 AND 2 THESSALONIANS were written to a congregation troubled not only by persecutions but by questions such as what became of those who died before Jesus came again, when will he come again, and what should Christians do until the Lord comes again. Paul's letters put these questions in their right perspective and give a great deal of practical common sense advice to earnest Christian people.

1 AND 2 TIMOTHY. Both of these Epistles are written under the name of Paul to a young pastor. The two letters deal with the kind of questions and problems that still arise in congregations and ministries today.

TITUS. This Epistle too was written under the name of Paul, ostensibly to a young pastor named Titus but actually to a congregation in Crete. Members of this congregation made the mistake of separating what they believed from how they lived.

PHILEMON is the most personal of the New Testament letters. Here Paul writes to a Christian in behalf of a runaway slave whom Paul has converted. What Paul asks for this slave is more than simple forgiveness. What Paul asks for the slave Onesimus requires Philemon to draw upon every bit of faith and faith-born courage of which a Christian is capable in any age or society.

HEBREWS. Is Christ better than the old Jewish religion and the law of Moses? Is the way of Christ worth enduring persecution? It was to answer these two questions that the tract often called the Epistle to the Hebrews was written.

JAMES. This so-called "Epistle" is not so much a letter or tract as it is a summary of the kind of life a Christian ought to live because of his faith in Jesus Christ. The emphasis of the book is upon being "doers of the word, not hearers only."

1 AND 2 PETER. Both of these Epistles are attributed to the disciple Peter. They were intended for Christians of Asia Minor

who not only faced severe persecution for their faith, but also had to struggle to keep their faith pure of false teaching.

1, 2, AND 3 JOHN. The first two of these general Epistles were written to encourage Christians in their faith against false teachers who taught that Jesus was a kind of invisible, ethereal spirit. The third Epistle bearing John's name commended a Christian named Gaius, who frequently had extended hospitality to missionaries in an age when hostels and inns were rare and often disreputable.

JUDE. One of the oldest false teachings abroad among Christians is the idea that because a Christian has been forgiven he can live and do as he pleases. It was to counteract this idea that this tract was written.

REVELATION. From the earliest times this book has been a playground for fanatics and unstable minds who have refused to read or understand the book in proper perspective. This book was not intended to be a program or schedule for the end of the world. Rather, this book was intended to bolster the hope and courage of Asian Christians during a time of very intense persecution. In order to do this the author uses many very vivid and powerful literary forms to convey the message that whatever happens in this world, God does not forsake and abandon his own, that God's victory will be ultimate and final.